SNAI

THE LIFE OF BOOBIE

LAWRENCE OF ACADIA

Lawrence Anderson

Artwork: Dr. Maha Eladwi

DEDICATION

To the memory of my mother Merdell Anderson

ACKNOWLEDGMENTS

My gratitude to friends and family who encouraged me to record some of my adventures as a child and grown up. My sincere thanks are extended to those who helped me through making this autobiography available in print.

As a little boy; I grew up in the city of LaPlace, Saint John the Baptist Parish; an extension or rather a suburb of New Orleans, Louisiana. We lived in the last house on a street we called "Blue Bird"; also known as 'Willow Street'. My grandmother, mother and aunts lived not far from each other. We raised a little herd of livestock; so to speak, in the yard; including chicken and one little pony.

One time, I grabbed a bucket to feed the pony. It tried to bite my hand. That was it for me with horses; in the back of the house.

There was also a hen house we called "A chicken coop." All those chicken and hens have to do; in order to earn their keeps, would be to lay their eggs within the coop, while the family would collect them as a stock for their meals.

One night, the chickens were startled and

made a big ruckus. We ran out to see what the noise was all about. There was a chicken that had been partially gobbled alive by some critter. We came to find out that it was a mink getting in the cage through a hole. We had to set a trap for the animal. We constructed a huge rat trap at the hole where the critter found its way in through to the coop. That was it for Mr. Mink.

Over the fence to the right side of our house was a man called "Mr. Mac". I am indebted to him for giving me the first job. I had to help him make money planting trees. My chores included punching holes in buckets and mixing soil and manure. It was a smelly mess; if you know what I mean! Mr. Mac and I traveled to other places moving trees back and forth as if I was working in a nursery. I had learned a lot, working for him.

The next day of my employ, we went in his garage to move a ping-pong table. Mr. Mac shouted: "'Tut' grab the other side". Tut was the name he gave me as he probably didn't care to check what people call me. To him, I was merely the boy next door. He did not care what to call me or how as long as I respond to

his instructions. He had a talent of making up names for people he knew or didn't know. Possibly my face or demeanor reminded him of King Tut.

Anyway, I went along to lift up the table from the other side. When the table was folded up it pinched my finger so bad that I went on screaming real loud. He took me to the doctor; they stitched me up. Since that day, Mr. Mac called me 'banana finger'. Though, I took the whole affair in stride. The trauma from that accident didn't stop me from working for Mr. Mac.

The day I got paid, my brother and I walked one or two miles along Fifth Avenue to the Clement's store in Main Street to buy some goodies. That was about how far the nearest realstore was to our home. We returned back home with heavy bags in our hands.

Coming back, there was a huge house with three big windows. One can easily see from the street, a large broom leaning on one of the windows. The broom brought to mind tales about the brooms witches ride to fly across and around to cause mischief to little kids like me. We heard many frightening and spooky stories about that particular house, which we have no clue of who lives there. Passing by those windows was very scary all around; especially in Halloween.

I think Dr. Robert Ory's father lived near that big house. I have known the Ory family for a long time. As a matter of fact, I watched his kids grew up to be Dentist just like him and his father.

Now back to telling the story about the eerie

broom house, which made us leery and wary whenever we approach it. We used to feel petrified whenever we just pass by the house during did light. when it gets dark, the surroundings become more frightening and spine-chilling. That could have been my pure imagination. However, when the night time approaches all I have seen were a lot of moving flying objects in the sky. That made me believe that what I am seeing was UFO's. I didn't know any better. It wasn't just one object, but there were many of them.

The mosquitoes were bad in our neighborhood. To deter the invasion of those little stinging creatures, we mowed the yard, put the grass in a stack then smoked the mosquitoes out. Everyone gathered around, played music and enjoyed the moment; we ended up doing that every weekend.

Next door to us was an old lady called "Ms. Deretta". She was a hard working lady herself. One evening, she had her brother come down from California. He was driving a customized Riviera that looked very much like the Cadillac car I had seen in the super fly movie. It was a beautiful car with a diamond window in the back, sunroof top, etc. The scene reminded me of the movie "Car Wash" and the song "Diamond in the Back" by Curtis Mayfield: "Diamond in the back, sunroof top, diggin' the scene with a gangsta lean Gangsta whitewalls, TV antennas in the back."

At the beginning of the lane there was a sweetshop and a barroom called "The Bluebird Night Club." I was too young to go in there from the front door, so I had to go in by the side door wherein I can get in unnoticed. My sisters and brothers loved me for that, because they were eating up the goodies I bring from the barroom. I loved seeing their thrill by what I get for them. I was taking care of my family at a young age.

In the 1970's there was an exotic place in LaPlace; called "the World Largest Snake Farm". It was the place where everyone who passes through our little town would stop by to see the Gorilla and a variety of snakes, boa constrictors, spiders and alligators. The owner used to supply medical centers with poisonous snakes venom to produce antidotes. Snakes around the bayous were poisonous and nasty; including rattlesnakes, and water moccasins (cottonmouth) and copperheads.

The gorilla stood up behind a huge glass that one can face it closely. In the corner there was a bubble gum machine for the spectators who like to play games with the gorilla and give it a treat. The customers place the gum in a hole for the gorilla to reach for the treat. If the gorilla's hand could not reach the gum, it would hit the glass and throw a ball of shit at

the spectator. To me, it was like the greatest show on earth during that time. Unfortunately the Snake Farm was shut down after Hurricane Andrews, in fear of inability to keep the critters in.

Down the street from the Snake Farm was the Frost Stop drive in; which is still in business today. We would go there to eat and then go home. For sweets there was "Mrs. Flossie Morris" sweetshop. She was selling all sorts of pies, pecan candy, praline, coconut candy and sandwiches. Now I know why our teeth became kind of rotten as we grew older!

In the trees; around our home, there was a huge owl that had lived long in the area. The owl had very big piercing eyes. It would scream like a hawk, whenever it hears our footsteps. That was a spooky, hair-raising feeling. The big bird used to run after us in our way home many

nights as if she is hunting a prey. That could have been a figment of our imagination. However, we have never stopped to check and verify.

On the other side of the street, there was the Robertson family home. We have often played with their kids.

It was around the Fourth of July, when we were playing with fireworks. Little Nolan was lighting the fire crackers and we gathered around to watch and hail. As a fire cracker goes off we get very excited with the blast! He did it again and again.

One time Nolan threw the fire cracker towards me without knowing where the fire cracker has landed. I looked around to track it for a split second; the fire cracker went off in my pocket. It blew my pocket out and burned my skin. Scared, I ran home fast, so fast. I felt as if my pants were on fire! My mother checked me out. I was angry from what Little Nolan had done to me. I went in my room to get my B.B. gun to get even, but my mother told me to back off. This incident taught me a lesson on how to watch out for any person who would try to hurt you.

I went to John L. Ory Elementary School, instead of learning I got in a little trouble fending off the critics. There was that huge guy called "Big West". My brother and I climbed on that guy's head and whipped his tail. The principal and the coach; Mr. Adams, brought me and my brother in front the class and paddled us both.

We went on to another school called Woodlawn School that was dominantly black. So there was a bigger task to fill, it turned out to be a fine school. I moved on from elementary to junior high school.

Many times; on the way to school, we would get on the school bus and some bully tries to make fun of my brother. We were not amused or having fun being ridiculed or bullied. It was one evening on a school day, as we were heading home, I got called out to meet some guy named Bobby on the tracks after school to fight. So, I let everyone know of what was about to happen. They all followed me as if I was the "African Rocky"! Then the fight began. We were throwing blows right and left. By the time, it was over; Bobby reached back to his friend who snuck him some brass knuckles. This didn't stop me though. We fought until he ran off. I had won the fight. As we were heading back off the tracks, I was rubbing my head as if I had hickies all over my neck; which I did! But for sure they were not love bites.

A little further up the street, there was the Loe family. The family members were acting like Cherokee Warriors! Whenever the weekend comes around, they would have a few barrels burning and pigs screaming! But that didn't stop me from intermingling with them. I met Mark and Beaver from that family. Then I got to know Kevin-lo and Yacht; just to name a few. Mr. Mule was the big daddy of the family.

Then there was the Jones family. They lived next to the Night Club. On a sunny Sunday, they were having a picnic; in mid-day, in front of the Bluebird Night Club. There were Harley bike riders doing tricks on their bikes, while the music was playing in the Club. I was fascinated by those bike riders or bikers.

My uncle Bubba was the DJ. I started working for my uncle, spinning records. My uncle went to places I couldn't go to because I was too young to hang around in the club. When he comes back he was drunker than Ned the wino.

The music started to get scratched up, so I started buying my own music. However, I have still accompanied him to a lot of events. I played the music while my uncle danced all over the place, climbed objects as if he were a gymnast. He used to call himself "The devil from underground".

My uncle had a battle with the DJ at Reserve Junior High School. I played the music and my uncle would dance around in his devil suit, climb up the basketball goal and swing from the rafters. He was energized!

At that school I played trumpet in the band. It didn't last long for me because my bladder was weak, so I came home pissing many times during the night. That was because the band director won't let you get out of the line, when you have to. That was the end of the band for me.

As I went to a reading class, there was a teacher named "Mrs. Clement". She lived in my neighborhood. She said to me once: "Lawrence I want you to read me a summary". So as bright as I thought I was! I got up and started to read what I had written. She looked at me and said, "Go and sit down!" The class broke all in laughter. I felt like she thought that I wasn't smart enough to be in her class. She realized that I was a friend of her daughter!

Leon Godchaux Junior High School was

the next school I had attended in 1979. That was an ancient school. Grass was growing through and around the bricks. It looked more or less like a college. The school was known for its talented football players, so Donald Carter and I went to join the team; not realizing that it was not anything thing like sandlot football, street football or backyard football.

I went in to practice, the coach yelled at the team to run in place, hit the ground and then jump back up. I looked at Donald and said: "that is it for me".

Instead of being a football player, I ended up working in the concession stand selling drinks, after the game was over.

One day, we had just won the game and I was going home. I didn't have a car at that time. I walked to the river road and stood there with my thumb out to catch a ride. Good thing I was paying attention because a truck was passing with a board sticking out the window. There was a ditch behind me, so I had to jump in to keep from getting hit in the face. I guess the truck occupants were mad because they lost the game.

Later on we were transferred to the new East St. John High School where I finished my high school diploma in 1981.

Time moved on and so did my family. We moved to a community called "Elm Loop", known as the "Brick City", wherein the population grew larger. There were a lot more friends to play with. We go to each other's house as if everyone were connected.

One Christmas Holiday we went to Miss Vickie house for the feast celebration. She had cooked some dirty rice which was nice and spicy. After we ate, we all gathered around to play a game of catch.

There was a pathway to the Keating's Grocery Store on Fifth Street. It was the store that everyone in our neighborhood goes to; not necessary as patrons of the store. Most guys sit under the trees for shade during hot summer days and eat hot smoked sausage with crackers and drink beer. The older guys would start off the day early in the morning; drinking and this would last into the night. It was the place where a handsome bum like me would hang out, not to just drink but to also seek wisdom. My wife used to come and get me away from the crowd; many times.

The place we called "Park Place" was just starting to develop and the road leading to it was a dirt road. We used to run around playing catch on a pile of dead trees we called "The Stock Pile". We keep on jumping and running around and about on the "Stock Pile" until I get exhausted. That is, when it is time to go home.

We played a game called "catch". Man! We did a lot of running and hiding from the catcher. We even leaped off of a two story complex; just not to get caught. We did not stop until getting dark at night.

Once, my brother Nolan and a couple of his friends were still on the top of the office building, after it became pitch-dark. My brother told me what had happened after the incident had occurred. He was sitting on a hard plastic sunlight bubble on top of the office. Then there was a loud thunder. My brother had fallen through the bubble. He came out through the door with his legs busted up! He got into big trouble for that.

The next day came. I just knew we were going to do something. I and Ape-pee Joe,

Porky, Warren, Daryl Clark, Nolan and Skipper; just to name a few, got in a mud fight against Wayne Fisher and his crew. We started by throwing mud at each other. So it happened that Wayne rose up to say "Throw me a rock, Throw me a rock". Skipper did what Wayne was asking for. It seemed as soon as he came up, the mud stroke his face and the game was over for that day. We grew up during the era of war games.

One morning, we decided to hunt for jobs together. We went to the Shell refinery, and worked for a contractor called "Brown and Root". It was a turn-around in that plant. Before we go to work we used to put all our food together in one big bag. We all ate in the same spot. That was the second job I had gotten. It was a better paying job too.

Then, I worked for the "Goodhope" refinery. That was the one plant wherein I did a lot of running. The funny part was that I was a fire watchman! However, I had to leave that job because it was too risky for me.

There was a man whose name was Bernard Jarrow, who was working on his car. I was curious about what he was doing and I was also fascinated by his car. I asked him: "can I give you a hand on working on this car". He said: "go get me a socket". Since then I knew I wanted to do mechanic work. Thanks to him. This was exactly what I did for him and continued doing.

The Tank: A Mustang I put together; Courtesy of the junkyard and a totaled vehicle

Another Mustang; getting a paint job - the product of genius creativity and hours of sweat and labor

I am the oldest of nine kids my mother "Merdell" had. I was very proud of her. My mother was the one who took in families to live with us. We lived in the back of the Project around the pine tree. For me there was all kind of activities to get into. My mother played cards, a game of spades, and even dominoes!

One of my brothers, Nolan had asthma, he was allergic to fish or any sort of seafood. There were times my brother uses the illness to his advantage. My mother fell for it; each time.

One day we were in the house throwing darts, he started to lose the game. I knew something was wrong, so I swiftly headed towards the other room. He threw the dart and hit me on the back of my leg. I ran to my mother, she yelled at him, but it didn't stop there.

The other time, our mother went on an outing, she had to come back because we were fighting over the television. That was the last time I and my brother got into a fight.

I remember when my step father "Earnest Bell" had brought me a blue 20" bicycle. It was the first bike I ever had. My mother told me not to go out on Elm Street with that bike. I said: "Ok mom I won't!"

Later, I was asked to go to the Keating Store, on Fifth Street; which was busy with heavy traffic; especially at the end of the morning shift in neighboring chemical and petro industry. I built up my courage to go, so I headed toward the store. I came out the Lane without looking for cars. Suddenly, there was a car coming at about 25 mph. The car

swerved to avoid hitting me. The back of the car hit me and my bike and tossed me up the air for about 5 seconds. Falling down, I hit the fence of a house. I knew, then that I was in trouble. Mr. Lennix came running down the street and told me to stay there. I felt like a ninja turtle. Scared as I was, I ran home without my bike and acted like nothing happened. Mr. Calvin who had hit me, brought my twisted bike home and offered me money to get it fixed. My mother asked me if I am ok, then she whipped my behind real good!

The accident took place by the St. Martin pharmacy. Dr. St. Martin was the pharmacist for our family. As I could recall he was the only pharmacist we knew of. I still see Dr. Tommy St. Martin once in a while and occasionally we have a chat.

Then, we started a bike group. We had some of the fanciest bicycles in the Parish. Warren was my best friend and we did a lot of things together. We rode in a bike marathon and made the headlines of the local newspapers. That publicity made me feel like a leader.

The other time, we were roller skating on the streets of LaPlace. We became very popular. My uncle borrowed my skates and didn't return them back for 3 days. Then, I learned not to let him use nothing of mine ever again.

My Uncle roller skating using my skates; a snap shot from a video

As I got older, my life started to change and so is the nature of the jobs I was interested in. I started working for Pine Construction; which was a contractor at the Marathon OIL Company. It was a laid back job; working 4 days a week and 10 hours a day.

It was a bright sunny day when I was getting in to work. Just as I was getting off, I went home to my mother's house, she ran to me holding me tight as if I was dead. She saw a news flash on TV and swore that they had said that I got myself killed. Everyone was in frenzy. I repeated "I am alive, I am Alive". It was pretty rough at that moment.

I had gotten married and had three wonderful sons, Lawrence James, III, Antoine and Traimone. I was living in Garyville at that time; not very far from LaPlace, but I couldn't stay away from my mother house.

I must have sensed something is going wrong with my mother. She was diagnosed with breast cancer. I had to step up to the plate because our father wasn't there to provide for us. It hurt for a while to see our mother vanish before our eyes, but we were stuck in it there together. We grew up and went our separate ways. We all lived nearby and no one moved out of the State except my youngest brother Michael, who went to the Service.

Playing the piano in Florida

As the years passed by, another tragedy struck my home. This time it was my youngest son Traimone. He was diagnosed with brain tumor when he was about four years old. His health started to deteriorate. The attending doctor at the Children's Hospital gave us the message: there isn't anything else they could do to cure him. He gave him a year to live. Then they granted him a wish: a place; of his choice, to go too. He chose to go to Disney World in Florida. We packed him up and the whole family flew up there. He had a ball out there. We rolled him around to almost every event. We stopped at the Hard Rock Café. After we ate; the kids wanted a banana split. The split was bigger than Traimone. We ordered one banana split for each one of them. The tourists were smiling and laughing to see how big the splits were. We got that week over and it was time to go back home. He was laid to rest a year later.

At that time, I was working for Sewell Plastics. I started working on the assembly line placing oil quart bottles on a slider. Often times, I toppled the bottles over. At one time, I put my arm to catch the fallen bottles. The moving belt caught my arm and squeezed it real tight. When my arm was released it was looking like Popeye's forearm, I never reported that incident.

My life has never been the same after my son's death. Stephanie and I got separated and I moved in with my sister Veronica for a while but not for long. It was a cold winter night, raining, when I left Garyville and got divorced.

I was single again, for a while. Then, one cold winter night at Gumbo's, the door opened and in walked Lavern. With her was a young lady I had never seen before. I asked Lavern to introduce her friend to me. Fabriell was her name. I asked her if she would like something to drink. She said she would like a coke. I gave her my phone number not knowing if she would call but she did so we started dating.

I didn't have a vehicle so I had to hitchhike my way to Kenner where she had lived. I visited her there. Later, I got a job working for National Rental Car at the airport; which was near where she lived.

Fabriell and I

My sons

I guess that coke went a long way, because Fabriell later became my second wife. We ended up having three kids together as well, Nicholas, Nathan and Nigel. Now, I have six grandkids Niya, AJ, Bree, Aniyah, Aubrie and Triamone and I love them all.

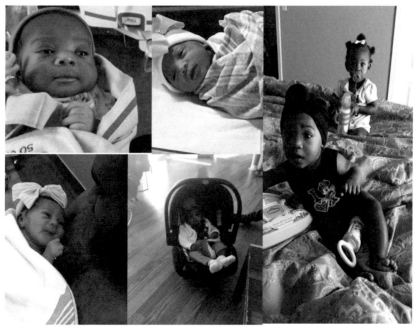

Snapshots of some of my grandchildren

My older granddaughter

Let me; now take you back to the time before my sons were born. It was 1992 when I was staying at my uncle's trailer. The weather was getting bad as hurricane Andrew was coming through. We didn't pay attention to what was going on as my uncle Bo-dilly and his friends were playing a game called Spades. They continued playing the game.

Suddenly the storm became serious. We could feel the pressure from the storm as it was coming through. The trailer was shaking and the windows were blown out. We all laid flat down on the floor for the ride. It was intense and we were scared. It would have taken our lives.

As the storm passed by, we got up to look out the door, the trailers were blown away and their debris was everywhere. From then on I have never taken a storm for granted. That was when my family started to flee when a storm is in the maling. The following day, you can see all the destruction the storm had left behind, the power was out, it was hard to get around in vehicles. It was like that for days or so.

Fallen tree and debris from the Tornado associated with Hurricane Andrew

Trees and the power lines during Hurricane Andrew

Home destruction; in LaPlace, from the Tornado
associated with Hurricane Andrew

After the cleanup, I went to other places
where help was needed; seeking work. I
stopped by the resident of Dr. Abdo Husseiny
and Dr. Zeinab Sabri at 132 Holly Drive in
the Riverland Estate. The couple has no
children. Dr. Zeinab's mother was coming to
visit them at that time and settled with them
since until Hurricane Katrina made its rounds.

Dr. Zeinab gave me the job for cleaning and
doing maintenance around their home, this is
how I became the "Care-Taker" for the
Sabri/Husseiny family. They give me the key
to their trust. It is like I became part of the

family and I have been ever since.

Then, I started working for Dr. Aziz Sabri; Dr. Zeinab's brother, as well. I mowed the lawn of his home on the week-end. He lived at the other end of LaPlace. The only problem I had; while working for Dr. Aziz was with his second wife; Samiha (Sam). She didn't like me too much. I didn't know her that well. She did not speak English very well, so maybe she didn't understand me or something.

There were one incident that took place when I was mowing the lawn, she made it seem like I was peeping at her through the rear window. When I heard the story about that I became very angry and started to dislike her. There were a few times I ran into her, when she was working in Wal-Mart. It happens that I go there looking for a shirt or something, then I see her in that department. When she spots me, she moves around as if I were stalking her. I knew something was wrong with her, then. I never saw her again; I think Aziz had divorced her.

Then there was Karen; his third wife. Aziz was a great man and probably didn't know this was coming. I think he met that woman in Mississippi. At times he took me on a trip to Bay St. Louis, Mississippi to her house. She had Aziz changing his life style for her. He told me to do whatever she wants.

Karen started buying furniture that I had to put together. That was a long day task for me. As time passed on, they decided to move to Mississippi.

Aziz was suffering from some sort of illness. She moved him away from all the help he had around him. He started to get frail after they got settled. Before you know it he was slowly dying. She told me my services were no longer needed.

Then, there was a time when my boss went to California for one month and a half. I would come over to check on "Nana"; the cat, to see if she had her food and water. I came to the house to check every other day.

One day I came in and there were Karen wandering around in the house. Karen said that she had a cell phone missing and she came to find out. It was more than the phone she was looking for. It was the 10,000 dollars under my boss's bed mattress. Dr. Zeinab had hid that money under the mattress for emergency. Later, Karen managed to say that I had taken it. I felt kind of heartbroken for all this time. I was taking care of them; they tried to pull a stunt on me like that.

Nana admiring the new wood floor that I supervised while my boss was in California

Meanwhile, I had a job working for Mr. Allen cleaning and repairing barges. We were broken up in teams; three to a group. My group included me (Boobie), Wayne and Green washing barges together as a team. We became one of the better crews. I moved up in the ranks in a matter of weeks. I loved the job so much. Once, I fell down in the river, came up and swam to the bank. Then, I went back in the water to get a tool I left behind. They thought I was crazy. After that incident, we were called "The River Rats."

I stayed on that job for about six years. One sunny evening; the boss of the company saw how hard I was working, he called me to the office and I was offered a supervisory position. I had to drive 32 miles to get there, and I did.

Going up North, I was the only African American working in a supervisory position. I had it kind of rough at first. Two of the supervisors were giving me hard time and causing me problems. At the end of the day, I reported them to the upper management. The boss came up there and straightened them out.

Christmas had come around, the company had a Christmas party we attended, Mark had come up with a game called "swing the grapefruit" game. Those were the good days, working for CGB.

I worked for that company for 14 years .Out of all those years, I worked on the river. I have witnessed things I had never seen before. There was this guy Joe. It so happened that I was coming around the barge to see

what is happening. Joe was eating rotten soy beans off the barge floor I asked him: "Joe what are you doing?" He said: "I am eating this for the protein". I damn near threw up and I couldn't wait to tell the other guys.

When lunch time came around, Chris and I were sitting together. Chris had some micro hot sauce he was playing with. I asked him to give me some. I put the sauce on Joe's 'poboy' when he walked off to get a drink. He came back to take a bite of the sandwich and started chewing. I can tell that the food was very hot. He stopped chewing and tried to drink water. It didn't help. I just knew, at that moment, I was going to lose my job.

Once there was an old guy named "Mr. Willie". I started to visit him. He had a lot of wisdom although people thought he has no brains. Nobody paid attention to him except for me. At the beginning of the month, I managed to bring him to the store to get little grocery and pay his bill. He used to grab himself a little bottle of whiskey to drink. We ride around for some time. When I come to a stop, he gets out of the car, looks at his watch and starts talking to it as if it was a walkie-talkie. I thought he was a conductor working for the railroad. I get him back into the car, take him home, unload off his grocery then I would quickly drive away.

We all of us lived near each other on Elm Loop, which we called 'Brick City'. We lived in an apartment in a quadruplex. Every weekend we had something going on; back there.

I had bought a 1970 Dodge Dart from Mr. Leroy. It was a nice car for me to clean up, so I did. That car drew to me a lot of attention and made me many friends. There was this one guy who called himself "Ice T." He would follow me everywhere I went with the car. It seemed as if he smells the car when it starts up. He was so cool. He would lay back and put his feet out of the window until the day my car had got into an accident. That was it for the joy riding at least for me.

It was a year's end, winter was in and I had no vehicle to ride. But, my so called friend bought himself one. I was looking forward to ride in his car like he did with me, but he proved me wrong. He had totally changed. I asked him to take me on for a ride; he decided

not to bring me around. I was stunned. I got mad. I asked him another day to do so and he bluntly declined. I felt very bad for being so humiliated. It was hard for me to swallow.

So, I sucked it up and realized that I couldn't get mad, but I could get even. As time moved on, he went to Texas and when he came back I had an F-150 truck. He saw me in the truck at the store while he was on a bike. He came over to me and said: "nice truck Boobie". That was when he opened his mouth to say: "Let's go riding some day."

Before he can finish, I told him: "I am giving rides to no one but my kids or it's me alone." I added: "those days are over buddy!" He pulled away on his bike and that was the last I have seen of him.

The race track

The following week, I gathered up my sons and drove them to the race track, we watched the races. When it was time to go, we started heading out. I drove the truck thinking I was heading towards home but I ended up in Mississippi! My kids were tired as they were crammed up. I finally stopped to get gas and drove back. It was about 2 am when I got home. My kids said they will never ride with me to the track ever again. So I brought them 3 Mongoose bicycles.

Nigel and I decided to go around the block for a bicycle ride. On the way coming back we got into a race. It didn't last that long. As we were coming around the curve, my front tire hit his back tire. Instead of me hitting the back breaks, I grabbed the front. The bike was stopped in its track and over the handle bars I went. I put my hands in front of me to keep my face from hitting the street pavement.

I looked over to the right side; there were people who gathered around, laughing at me. I got up with my crooked handle bar, and rolled the bike home looking like an imbecile who doesn't know how to ride a bike. It was embarrassing and it took me about 3 weeks to heal.

Summertime came around. It was time to mow the lawn. The "Husseiny" family gave me a lawnmower and a pressure washer. I went to work cutting Abdo's grass. As I was getting to it, there was a dark spot on the ground. When I passed over the area it seemed like a cloud of smoke but instead it was fire ants coming out of the ground. I looked down at my pants; there were fire ants all over my pants. I ran around the house so fast, you would've thought my pants were on fire. I had to wait until the fire ants settle down because the lawnmower was in their territory.

On the following day, my boss called me, I was just getting off from work, and he said "Cookie;" a black cat that preceded Nana, was missing. So I started to look for it. I was all over in the neighbors yards; yelling for it. She wasn't nowhere in sight.

I went back inside to say: "hey boss, I don't see her!" So I went back through the garage, I can hear her meowing. She was on the roof looking out to the street, terrified! I got a ladder and climbed up to reach for it. She swung and hit my fingers as if she was giving me five. Her claws scratched my fingers and I damn near fell off the ladder. So I climbed down and said to her, since you scratch me you are sleeping up there! It took me a little while to get her down, but I had gloves on me that time. Then, I decided to open the window to let her in.

Let me take you back a little.

I went for a ride with my best friend; Warren Watkins a.k.a. "Amp Scamp", on Airline Highway in his Oldsmobile; that he put together. We stopped at a store to pick up something to drink and cigarettes. I had never smoked before, so I asked him to let me try a puff. That was how I picked up that habit. I got dizzy. After a mile or two, he said; passing me a bottle of alcohol: "have some". I just knew there was nothing to it. So I took a swig. I started feeling mellow so I had a little more. We were jamming to the music and my head started to feel heavy. I was feeling the booze sneaking in and working on me. I laid my head back enjoying the ride, while my eyes were closed.

I got drunk and my friend was cooking up something for me. As we were going down New Sarpy Road, I can feel the car going faster. He yelled "Boobie" and jumped the track. In a second we were airborne inside the car. When we came down and hit the street, I thought I had swallowed my tongue. He burst out laughing. I opened the door, fell out of the car and threw up all over the ground. He pranked me good on that one.

My best friend Warren or Amp Scamp was from Germany. His family, Mr. and Mrs. Watkins, Porky, Chub and the late Squeaky were fisherman. His dad would go out and come back with a lot of fish and shrimp, if we needed some seafood they were the ones to go to.

Another time, I rode with Amp Scamp when he was driving his Dad's Ford Galaxie or LTD car. We were driving down Airline Highway, Porky was in the front and I was in the back. There was laundry and detergent in the back sitting next to me. For all I know we were going to the Laundromat. My friend must have taken his eyes off the road because he suddenly slammed the brakes and we slid into someone's car. The hit was so hard. It pushed the seat and jammed Porky into the dash board and broke his nose.

The police came to assist in the accident. Warren must have called his Dad because Mr. C came to the scene. I don't know what his Dad told the state police. I saw him throw his dad against the car, cuffed him and shoved him into the car with his feet. The cop looked like he weighted no more than 110 pounds.

That was something I had never seen and have never expected. It had looked like something out of the movies.

One sunny weekend, we all gathered up to go to the spillway. We all went to a water pond; Cardell, Amp Scamp, Daryl Clark and a host of other guys. Warren had taught me how to swim a little. "Come on in guys the water is great"; Warren said! Cardell was the second one to jump in, knowing he can't swim. The water was deep in some places. He walked around in the pond and then went off the edge. Right there he proved it. Warren knew he couldn't swim so he said to me: "Go help him!" I jumped in the water as if I was a life guard. Cardell grabbed me and pulled me down with him. I just knew he was going to drown me. I fought him off. He went under in a panic. Warren jumped in and saved him. Today he lives to tell the story.

The following day, we ended up at a swimming park called "Regala Park". It has a 12 feet pool. I recall myself getting on the board to jump. I underestimated the spring board. It was flexible. As I hit it, I went up and came down like a cannon ball splashing

into the water! I knew they were watching me, so I stayed under and swam to the 4th feet mark.

I couldn't see the snow white bottom of the pool. The pool was so clean, my face scraped the bottom of the pool and I came up with a burn on my face. Boy! Did they laugh at me! I walked around with scrapes on my face for a week.

A week past; I called my brother Nolan, Tettie Bum, and a few other guys; asking them: "Hey guys let's go and get some pecan". So we started out to the orchard. We all had our little bags. We knew we were going to get some pecan and we did. It was getting so good until a man came galloping on a horse. We took off running down the track. The man was keeping up with us so we turned into a field. However, Teetie Bum screamed out, crying in fear, "I am stuck on the fence". So I took 5 steps back and knocked him down off the fence. We got up and started running through the field.

My brother had a tear in his bag. I don't know which way the other guys went. All I saw was 3 of us running! I still had my bag. We made it across the long field. The man dismounted the horse and jumped in a truck trying to cut us off. I was so tired; I jumped across the fence and went over the levee. I lied down on the grass and said: "If he came over here, he can have these pecans!" As I was gasping for air, I waited for about 10 minutes then I started running behind the levee until I got home. We got our ass whipped for that!

My younger brother; Mikey came home from the Navy Base. He said: "let's go fishing big brother". I said: "let us do it!" I just knew there were stipulations; once I agreed. He said the one who catches the least number of fish, carry the bucket! Back then I was crazy enough to go for it. We started walking down the long track by the lake, and then we started fishing. The fish were biting pretty well and he was catching them quickly.

I started sweating, knowing that I was going to carry the bucket. Then, the fish started to come my way. I was pulling them in fast; as well. The getting was so good, I pulled my line in that time, and there were a snake holding onto my fish. I then knew it was time to go! I looked at the bucket and said "damn!" I thought about that long ass track. We were about to walk all the way and I had that heavy bucket to tote.

I was sweatng bullets when we got to the car. I didn't worry about going on that trip too much afterward. My brother; Mikey, brought himself a boat since then.

Let me tell you a story about a dog called Jack. The dog was named after my uncle "Black Jack". It was my uncle's dog but it followed me all around as if it was mine. Whenever I call "come Jack"; it wags its tail and comes before me. It would listen sometimes.

Across the street, there were some stray dogs living under a bar room called: "The Shack". When you pass by that place, the dogs start barking at you as if they own the road access rights and do not wanting you to pass. Since I had Jack following me through the passageway, the dogs came out after Jack. He acted as if he was so bad fighting with the dogs.

Black Jack looked like a prize fighting dog too, until one day I came out to my grandmother's house. I went back in the house and came through the back. Jack didn't see where I went. I was peeping from the back of the house to see what Jack was doing with the stray dogs. There was one dog that looked like a wolf. Its teeth showed a big under bite. The wolf-like dog looked kind of scary. It walked toward Jack with a vicious growl. In disbelief, I watched Jack lay down and the hostile dog was all over it. Jack wouldn't give the dog a fight, while it was pounding on it. I came from behind the house; Jack jumped up and acted like it wasn't afraid. I knew then that my dog was a coward.

The following day I was going to the store. So I started walking on the road heading toward Airline Highway. Jack was leading the way, I yelled: "Go back Jack!" It turned around like it was going back to the house. As I continued to walk; Jack figured out how to get ahead of me, there it was again trotting in front of me; as if I told it to come. I yelled at him again: "go back home Jack!" It moved back with its tail down, then I threw a rock at it. It started running back or at least, that what I have thought. I came out of the store heading back home. When I got there, I started looking and calling for Jack. There was no sign of Jack. It wasn't there!

The next day came; the neighbors told me

that they saw Jack on the side of the Airline Highway. It had been hit! I broke into tears, thinking that it went back home. It took me quite a while to get over Black Jack.

Then, there was the softball season, the night club had formed up a team called "The Shakers". That was one of the funniest teams that I had ever seen. It started out looking like they were going to be something significant, then things started to change. They would drink booze, go out and practice, play and lose the games. No matter what happened, they act like they were winners because when they get back, the booze was waiting on them. They party all the time. There were some good players and things. On Sundays there was a baseball tournament on Woodland School ground. All sorts of baseball players were out there. It was the place to be at that time.

Then there was Wade, Warren and me. We built a bicycle ramp to jump off. As I got to jump off the ramp from the ground, Wade was running his mouth. I was going as fast as I can up the ramp. When I came off the ramp I soared 6 feet into the air, came down and I landed perfect. It felt so good. I did it again.

Wade went after that, he came around the house coming to the ramp at full speed! In the middle of the jump the chain came off the bike, he was airborne without the bike. He hit the ground screaming: "Ooh! aah!" It was so funny. It just didn't stop there. Wade didn't get enough.

There was a guy called Hammerhead. He had a sport Chevrolet Camaro car and a Kawasak ZRX1100. The car was so clean, I couldn't help but to admire it. One day he came out on his bike and Wade asked him for a ride around the block. As he was holding on, Hammerhead had slightly hit the throttle; and there were Wade again on the ground. He was burnt up from scraps and cuts. He must have told the man to hit the throttle! I can tell you these stories happened as if they were just yesterday.

Then there were a time when I, Warren, Brain, Mark, Beaver and Porky; just to name a few. We were on our way toward the levee to go hunting. Before we got there, there was a fence to climb. Mark went across the fence; first. Ricky climbed the fence next, and then he reached for the rifle and pulled it over the fence. The butt of the gun hit the ground and went off. Ricky was shot in the stomach. It happened so fast. We cried in fear. His mother came over to check on her son. She didn't know how it happened. She thought Mark had shot him! She blamed Mark for a long time for that. It was the last time I ever went hunting and it was the first time I had ever seen a friend die on the scene.

As I am sitting here jotting down my thoughts and memories, I often think about the golden days when there was little bad blood among people, not like the way it is today.

There was another incident when I and four other guys got off from work in Convent. As we were making our way home, the police pulled the three guys over, got them out of the car to the ground, as I passed them. I pulled off near them to assist. The police yelled at me: "get back in your truck". I yelled to the guys: "I am going to get help!" I drove away with my foot stuck to the pedal running to their home to tell their parents. I came to work the next day, they said the police mistook them for someone else. It was a good thing. It was daylight, who knows what could've happened!

Let me take you back to hurricane Katrina in 2005. I was living down the English Colony in Cambridge when the storm went through. We knew the storm was coming for sure, so we decided to leave at the last minute. The place had looked like a ghost town. Everyone had left and got out of the neighborhood.

I hit Airline Highway; heading up north while the traffic was so jammed up. We were stuck on the highway like a pack of sardines. We also had a dog named Akahia. It was a hot day and we weren't moving that much. When the traffic did move, we ended up somewhere in Mississippi! Just to be lucky, there was a shelter we pulled up to. It was a little crowded, so I walked my family inside to get settled and then I slept in the car with the dog. The night passed!

It was daylight when we started heading

back to see what had happened to our home. There was a road block! The National Guard was checking the traffic and they were only letting the residents back in. When we got to our home, the power was out, the trees were down, some streets were blocked, and there was no running water! When night time came, it was so dark that you can see stars you have never seen before.

There was a car light coming down the street. It was my wife's family coming down the street like they were on vacation. So we made room for them to stay. The house was very hot! I decided to set up a tent outside for the kids to sleep in. We used burning candles for light. The others stayed in the hot house. I decided to sleep on the lawn chair.

On the next day, I went to see my uncle home down Orange Loop. Their house moved off the foundation and ended up into the street.

I went to Home Depot to get a generator all the way in Gonzales, the store was packed! The lines were long. I felt a little relief when I got back home, because the generator supplied power to the fans and the deep freezer.

As days had passed, it seemed like we were going to be out of power for a while. It was damn near a week before the power finally came on in the evening.

I couldn't wait to see the news and the damage the storm had caused! The next few days the water started to rise from the lake and flooded our streets. The water smelled kind of raw. Turning on the news we learned that there were people stuck on roofs and bridges. It was a total mess. People were displaced.

I had an uncle called Bodilly; who was also displaced. We called around to find him at no avail. We got no response from him. No one knew where he was.

It so happened to see the news and he was getting on a bus to Texas. It took a while before I got in touch with him. I was told that he was living with some friends he met along the way. My grandmother finally got in touch with him and gave him my number. He called me; but before he could say anything, he said: "send me some money". I asked him: "Are you ok?" He said "Great nephew!" I hung up the phone on him.

I thought that it was pretty absurd for him to not call his family. It was a disaster and a lot of people were found dead. It was a sad time for Louisiana but we are resilient!

On one sunny day, my brother Nolan and I were playing around, looking at squirrels running around the tree. My brother said to me: "Watch me throw and hit a squirrel". Just like that. He said he hit the rodent and it was knocked out. So it seemed! He picked it up by the tail and put it in a bag. The animal came back to life. It cut through the bag with its razor sharp claws and attacked him. Boy! Did I break out running and laughing! He was lucky that the squirrel didn't stay on him. I guess we couldn't eat that one. Some do.

I had bought a 1970 Mercury Montego from my cousin Melvin. It was a nice old car. I had a little problem with it though. The transmission went out, so I put another one in. It was a bigger one. The shifting cable was not aligned up, so I cut a hole in the floor board and put a 3 foot rod in it; as if I was driving an 18 wheeler! I placed a rag into the hole to keep the heat from coming into the car.

One night, after I parked the car, someone knocked on the door and said: "Your car is smoking." I jumped up and ran out. Sure enough the car was smoking. I opened the door and pulled out the rag. It had me worried for a minute, but this didn't stop me. I replaced it with a wet rag and kept on riding.

Then there was a time; Jackie and I were playing chicken with the cars. He went to the opposite side of the road and so did I. He became scared and crossed back over and we had a head on collision. My car was fine but he had to show my sister how he messed up her car.

One evening, I was getting off from work, Abdo called me to come over, so I went to see what was going on. He locked himself in the house! I thought it was a fire or something. It was the maid who was taking care of his home. She was roaming around the house. He had locked her out and she was holding him inside like he was a hostage! I went to the back of the house where she was. I said to her, "Calm down and tell me what happened?" After I found out, I asked her to leave before she gets in trouble. She was acting as if she was "love struck". He must have felt sorry for her because she was back the next day.

Abdo's family members started to come and spend some time with him. They would stay a month or two at a time. I usually go to the airport and get them like an Uber driver.

First it was his sister-in-law and her son. However, she rents a car. Her son and I would talk about the last time he came. Abdo's sister-in-law would send me to the store to shop. She tells me: "If you don't get my cigarettes I am going to kill you". I make sure I get her the right ones all the time!

When Abdo's nephew is around, they order lobster, fry fish and eat soft shell crab.

Then, they laugh and joke around; on the patio, smoking hookah. By me taking care of them, there has never been a dull moment in my life. When days pass and it is time for them to go back to their home, I load up their luggage and greet them off. Then, I go back to my normal duties of taking care of Abdo.

It was September. Here come Dr. Abdo's young brother and his wife. I go to the airport to greet them and bring them to Abdo's home. I unload their luggage and get them settled in. The next day I start my journey off bringing them to the mall. Sometimes, I have to drop them off in separate places and they give me a certain time to come back and get them. This stuff goes on for sometimes until they leave. The brother makes a plan for me to come back in a few hours to bring him to New Orleans and drop him off in Bourbon Street for a few hours then I come back to take him home. This continues through the week. It was like I am taking them on a tour. His wife collects all sorts of clothes, shoes and trinkets to bring back to their home.

Now it's a new year and Mardi Gras has arrived. Abdo's older brother and his wife come to visit around that time. I go to the airport to pick them up as well, get them to Abdo's home, off load their baggage and get them settled in. When it is Lent season. I drove Mohamed to mass on Fridays, drop him off and come back and get him. Afterwards we go to the Arabic store to get organic food and spices. Once we get home while his wife is already in the kitchen preparing their dinner. They don't go out as much, but they sure know how to re-arrange the kitchen!

I come in the next morning to help Abdo, put his socks and shoes on for him. When I go into the kitchen I find the sink full of dishes. I didn't mind so much. I clean it up and put the dishes back where they belong. I leave out and come back within two hours; the dishes are back in the sink. I just knew they thought that I was from Egypt. Ok, I wash them again. It was later in the day so I left for that day. The following day the mess kept repeating itself, so I pulled the brother to the dishwasher and I said this is where the dirty dishes go. He looked at me as if he didn't know what I was saying. As time went by, they started to get better with cleaning up behind themselves.

Then that brother decided to go outside to the backyard and do agriculture work around a 300 year old oak tree! He put the shovel to the ground and decided that he couldn't dig around the tree. He came to get me to do it. I put the shovel to the ground and saw the roots in the ground like a spider web. I said "Sir, you cannot dig around the tree". He insisted on trying to plant the trees in that area. We ended up cutting the bottom of the plant pot and place them at the base of the tree.

The time passed by, it was time for them to head back to their son in another state. I loaded them up, hug and waved them off, they will be back soon. I have been taking care of this family for a long time.

Then, there was the son of an old friend of Abdo. He was a Professor of Medicine, surgeon and a Heart specialist. I picked him and his family up from the airport and drove them to Abdo's home. Off, I unloaded their luggage. It was less than an hour; his wife and daughter were running from Nana. I knew that they didn't want to stay there. So, I turned around and grabbed their luggage and drove them down town. It took a while for them to get settled in. For some reason Abdo's acquaintance did not like the hotel they checked in. I ended up getting home a little late that night! I had to double back; the following morning, to pick him up to bring him and drive him to Abdo's house for breakfast. I did some driving on that day! We ended up at Fernier restaurant by the Lake. Abdo's acquaintance and his family didn't stay very long. Thw wife went to the ticket booth to get a refund. We left out and came back to get her, she wasn't there! It was like someone lost in a crowd of people. We waited around for her to return. We were at the airport in a few hours, then we said farewell to each other and they went on their way.

Just recently, we went to my grandmother Mariah's birthday party, she is 92 years old. I hadn't seen my grandmother in months. Oh, but when I did, her face lit up like a Christmas tree and I was glad to see her too. I gave her a birthday present and told her, "I'll be back a little later to the party".

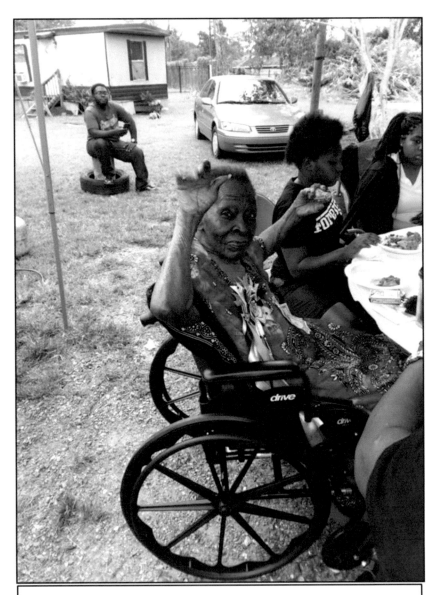

My grandmother Mariah

My grandmother was at the table when I returned back. She was having a good time with the family. Richard a.k.a. Booger Man asked our grandmother to give him the money off her dress. My grandmother put her hand on the money as if she wanted to back slap him. She is protective of her money. We still maintain the old fashion Southern tradition of clipping gifts of banknotes of different denomination to the dress of the birthday girl. This is in lieu of gifts that she may not like or has no need for.

Our grandmother was real delighted to see everyone at her gathering.

As the time passes, so does our age. My boss Abdo is old and starting to have problems with his knee and legs. I come in to check up on him daily. One day he is ok and other times he is not feeling good. I try to get him to go to the doctor; he says "I will go".

We sit down together and he tells me about the places he has been to. I get excited when he tells me how things are in the other kingdom. Or, we talk about different types of Egyptian food. He had me cooking all kinds of meat. I bake lamb ribs and tried it for the first time. Now he has me eating blue cheese, it smells kind of cheesy, but I got adjusted to

it. I take him to his appointments and bring him back. Sometimes we stop at a place to get a bite to eat. There is nothing I won't do for my boss Abdo. He inspired me to write this book, even when I thought I couldn't do it.

This is good time for me to tell you how I became ill. I thought I would never get to this part but I did. One evening, Mr. Cedric and I were coming for a delivery. I was raising my arm to stop the pain, but it continued to get intense. I reached to the back of my head and pressed in, I couldn't stop the pain. So I went to the urgent care to see what was going on, the test came back. I was diagnosed with an enlarged heart. I thought I was strong, but my heart wasn't.

We would go to the games and I would tell them: "I will catch up", knowing I was having a breathing problem. I went to the doctor to get a defibrillator put in my chest.

After I became well; at least I thought I was, I tried to work in Marathon, I passed the test for the job and went in with my tools to work. I wondered why it took so long for them to put me in the field. One of the foremen came and told me that there was a problem with my health. I worked three days with them, and then they let me go.

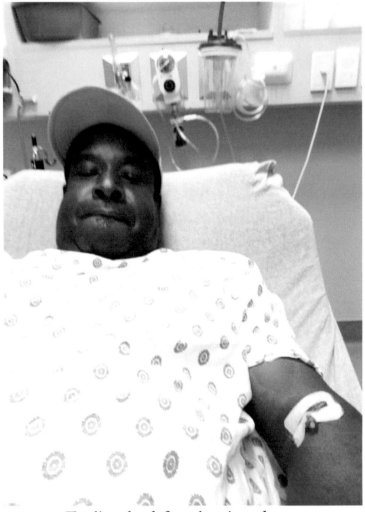

Feeling bad for slowing down

I worked all my life. It was hard to go out like that with heart problems. It brought tears to my eyes! I just knew my life was over. By the grace of "God" I am here today to tell you my life story.

Ok, let me take you back to the time when my father-in-law Bo-Willie came to visit my kids. We had a problem up stairs! We went up to see what the shouting was about, there was a bee flying around the ceiling. He climbed out on the ledge to see where the bees are coming from. There was a nest over his head. As he was trying to get back through the window, the bees landed on him like "jam on bread". They were stinging him as they were swarming in the house. We closed the door on him and fell out laughing!

There was another time when I bought a treadmill to exercise on. I put it together and tested it. I had to leave and go out for a moment. I explained to them not to get on the machine. However, my son Nathan was being curious!

When I came back from my outing, I got a report that Nathan had got onto the machine, put the key on and pressed the number 5 to walk on it. He was walking for a moment then it started to gain speed! He couldn't keep up. It threw him off like a rocket! His mother woke up from the loud boom. He jumped up like nothing happened!

On this bright Sunday, mid-day there were Wan-e, Duck and I. Wan-e said: "Hey Boobie come and help me get the cow in the trailer". I was crazy enough to say: "Ok, let us do it". We were in the pasture chasing a bull around the field. I said to Wan-e in a laughing manner: "We are not going to catch the bull and bring him to the cage!"

As we were running behind the bull, it ran to the fence and leaped over it. I was laughing so much and out of breath at the same time. I could not keep up with them. I don't know how he caught the bull because I left them out there.

I hope that this story of my life will give you an idea of what I have gone through. You may learn a lesson or two. You may relate the funny situations to your youngins to amuse them and teach them how to jump off a hot seat.

One morning I was getting ready for work. At that time, the socks were in a bag in the closet and the room had carpet on the floor.

So I stretched out on the floor, my body was halfway in the closet. It seemed as if something had happened to me because my wife Fabriell got up and saw me lying there without moving. She thought I was dead on the floor. She was yelling: "Lawrence". I had scared her out of her wits. I jumped up and laughed; it was so funny at the moment.

I have a brief story of my brother Nolan. My brother grew up wanting to be a policeman. He did everything that was required for him to get there, by any means necessary! My brother was a black belt in karate, was as good as any other cop. He was good to the community and did whatever he could to help his fellow man.

Nolan once took me and slammed my ass in the cop car. I had deserved that one. He was going to take me in. I was acting like a man out of control! We had a "man to man" talk; then, he let me go. I didn't look at him as my brother, but as an officer of the law. He was one of the officers that would give you a chance to straighten yourself up. We did a lot of things growing up together. I won't get involved in his personal business, but I would take a ride with him to listen to what he had on his mind. Other times, I would not be there for him. He gave me the name "Uncle Tom". I truly miss my brother; may he "R.I.P".

My brother Nolan

I got a call one day! I was at work and he was in trouble, I raced to get to him but the officer of the law sent me on a wild goose chase. I could not understand at that time why they wouldn't let me save him or give me a chance to talk him and calm him down. As the time passed by, I look at the picture and understand why he wasn't coming back from that incident.

As I set here writing in this autobiography, sometimes I wonder! Is this going to work for me! This is my first book I wrote. I wreck my brains to come up with the things that I did in my life.

Today, I went out to get some dog food and I ran into some old friends that I told them about a story I included in the book. When I told them about it, each one of them said, that sure did happen!

One evening I was cooking for Abdo and the crew of a young lady friend of his arrived. He treats her as a granddaughter; he has never had and she has adopted him as a Dad. He enjoys her company and the presence of her children. They give him the sense of family with all its merits.

Often, she brings her kids and the neighbors' kids with her to pay Abdo a visit. She had a son and two daughters. When the food was finished, everyone gathers at the table to eat except for the son. He wonders around as if he was up to something. Then I found out what was it, he was after. The Sponge Bob Popsicle! He always wanted to close the garage door when I leave; so I let him do it. Just so happened I had to re-open the garage door and there he was standing there as if he was a deer when the car light shined on him.

Abdo's friend has a pattern of trying to do things quickly, until one day her young daughter shut the glass sliding door to the other room; for one reason or the other. The mother was moving so fast she didn't realize the glass door was closed. Without a thought, she walked into the glass without seeing it closed and almost cut her head off! Sometimes being in a rush can cause injuries and of course. I had to clean the mess up.

Every other weekend I would go to Restaurant Depot to grab some items for her and Abdo to cook for that day.

I thank God for waking me up daily to go and do my job, taking care of Abdo and his extended family.

ABOUT THE AUTHOR

The author; Lawrence Anderson aka Boobie, Tut and Uncle Tom is a resilient man who graduated from the University of Hard Knocks with flying colors. There he had real education and hands-on training. Although there is no age-limit for graduation, he graduated at young age and he sooner had learned the theory of success. His charming personality and demeanor made him popular and gained him many friends. To his credit he practically knows everyone in the small town wherein he grew up and flourished.

ABOUT THE ARTIST

The artwork as well as the cover design of this autobiography is provided by Dr. Maha Eladwi; a fashion designer and scholar. Her unique style and pen strokes are embodied into the sketches and illustrations that visually portray particular events and situations. Her clever depiction uses art as an international language that can be grasped by everyone regardless of age, education level or linguistic upbringing.

ABOUT THE ENVIRONS

LaPlace is the seat of St. John the Baptist Parish, Louisiana, United States. The St. John the Baptist Parish Police Jury decreed in 1971 that the official spelling of the town includes a capital letter "P". This probably gives some people the notion that LaPlace is named after the famous French mathematician.
LaPlace is situated along the East Bank of the Mississippi River, in the New Orleans

metropolitan area. The population was 32,134 at the 2010 census.

LaPlace is the southern terminus of Interstate 55, where it joins with Interstate 10, and of US 51, where it terminates at the junction with US 61; Airline Highway. LaPlace is located 25 miles west of New Orleans.

Historically, the Chitimacha lived in the LaPlace region prior to the arrival of the

Europeans. The tribe's lands once encompassed the entire Atchafalaya Basin, westward to Lafayette, Louisiana, southward to the Gulf of Mexico and eastward to the New Orleans area. The Chitimacha Tribe currently resides on a reservation in St. Mary Parish, Louisiana.

Present-day LaPlace was settled by German immigrants in the early 18th century during Louisiana's French colonial period, as part of a larger settlement on the bank of the Mississippi called Karlstein; which was one of the four settlements collectively known as the "German Coast" (La Côte des Allemands), having been populated by German-speaking immigrants since 1721. French and Acadians intermarried with the Germans, and the area came to be known as Bonnet Carré (square bonnet). The name Bonnet Carré was inspired by the right-angle turn of the Mississippi river near the settlement and its resemblance to a square bonnet. Manual Andry built the Woodland plantation in 1793, and cultivated sugarcane. The crop was lucrative if brutal methods were used, as had been common in Haiti (and had led to a successful slave rebellion there). In early January 1811, slaves at Woodland Plantation and several nearby plantations attempted the German Coast Uprising. A group of 200-500 slaves armed with guns, axes, and cane knives set out from LaPlace to conquer New Orleans and gain freedom for themselves and others. Local white militia men crushed the rebellion within three days, and nearly 100 slaves were killed in battle, slaughtered by pursuing militia, or executed after summary trials by planter tribunals. Although more slaves may have participated in the Black Seminole rebellion in 1836 and the whole of the Second Seminole War, this is now considered the largest slave rebellion.

In 1879, pharmacist, planter, and patent medicine purveyor Basile LaPlace arrived from New Orleans, and established a large plantation in Bonnet Carré. In 1883 he allowed the New Orleans and Baton Rouge Railroad to cut through his land. The settlement's railroad depot was named after LaPlace, then the post office, and eventually the town itself.

In the 1920s, the Woodland Plantation was bought by the Montegut family, but the most famous person born there may have been Kid Ory, who was born in an outbuilding and later led a successful New Orleans jazz band.

The Andouille Festival

The Swamp

Evergreen Plantation

San Francisco Plantation

Whitney Plantation

LaPlace Airport

Made in the USA
Columbia, SC
21 April 2025

56974158R00058